Basher Science™

EXTREME WEATHER

KINGFISHER

First published in 2023 by Kingfisher
an imprint of Macmillan Children's Books
6 Briset Street, London EC1M 5NR
Associated companies throughout the world
www.panmacmillan.com

EU representative: 1st Floor, The Liffey Trust Centre,
117-126 Sheriff Street Upper, Dublin 1 D01 YC43

Text and design copyright © Toucan Books Ltd 2023
Illustrations copyright © Simon Basher 2023
www.basherscience.com

Author: Tom Jackson
Consultant: Dr Peter Inness, University of Reading
Editor: Anna Southgate
Designer: Dave Jones
Proofreader: Richard Beatty

Dedicated to Sebby & Remi

ISBN: 978-0-7534-4829-8

A CIP catalogue record for this book is available
from the British Library

Printed in China
9 8 7 6 5 4 3 2 1
1TR/1122/WKT/RV/128MA

MIX
Paper | Supporting responsible forestry
FSC® C116313
FSC
www.fsc.org

CONTENTS

Introduction
Natural Disaster

If you're lucky, you will only ever see me in a movie or on the news. I hope so – but the truth is, I'm appearing more often year on year and that's going to make me harder to avoid in the future. I storm in as thunderous downpours that swamp cities, or swarms of whirling wind that rip buildings apart. Or perhaps I'm busy baking and burning up the land, leaving nothing but scorched earth in my wake. In many ways I'm nothing special – I come about because of the weather. But this is not normal weather I'm talking about, this weather is *extreme*.

You see, I've struck up a close connection with Climate Change, particularly the kind that is caused by you humans. It's your use of fossil fuels, among other things, that is causing Climate to change. Read on to learn more about the hows and whys of this. Please don't ignore me – but you shouldn't get down about me either. There are things you humans can do to make me less of a disaster. Get it right, and I might start to show up less often. Fix things while the sun shines, they say, so you're prepared for the rain, hail and wind when it comes . . .

Chapter 1
Climate Crew

Come rain or shine, we're the high rollers who influence the weather across the globe. We take our lead from Sun, who feeds us with the energy we need to mix things up and make a difference. That is what we are all about: differences. We thrive when hot smashes into cold and dry clashes with wet. This is what creates Weather System. Nowadays the weather we churn out day after day, year on year, is becoming more extreme. Just check out the characters that make up the Windbags, the Water Monsters and Great Balls of Fire to see what we mean.

Sun

Seasons

Weather System

Climate

Climate Change

Climate Model

Sun

■ Climate Crew

☀ This mega fireball supplies our planet with heat
☀ Provides all the energy needed for weather to occur
☀ Trapped solar heat is causing climate change

Rise and shine! Things are hotting up, and that is because my blazing starlight provides all – yes, all – of the heat energy that creates weather down there on your little planet. Without me there would be no more sunny days, for sure, but also no wind, no rain, no clouds.

You see, what you call weather happens when a warm mass of air crashes into a colder one. My hot sunlight heats up some parts of Earth while other areas grow cold. When air masses coming from the two meet, things can get a little stormy. All of this is natural, but Climate Change has started hoarding my heat. Now, when air masses clash, the differences between their temperatures are growing ever larger. And that can only mean one thing . . . Yep, weather is becoming more extreme!

● Surface temperature of the Sun: 5700 °C
● World's sunniest place: Yuma, Arizona (12 hours of sunshine a day, on average)
● 173,000 trillion watts of solar energy hit Earth every second

Sun

Seasons
■ Climate Crew

☀ A four-step cycle of changing weather
☀ Change occurs due to Earth's tilt going around the Sun
☀ Causes weather to swing between extremes each year

We are a cycle of weather changes that signal the passing year: winter, spring, summer and autumn. To understand us better, take a sideways look at Earth. You see, the big blue-green beauty is leaning over as it spins on its axis. As this planet rolls around Sun each year, the top half – the northern hemisphere – leans nearer to the hot star. Then, as the months pass, it swings away again, and the southern hemisphere takes its turn to face Sun.

Leaning in to Sun creates a summer of long, hot days and steamy nights. Leaning away makes a winter of short, gloomy days and chilly nights (brrrr). When it's summer up north, it is always winter down south. Spring and autumn share the sunshine equally across the globe, either warming up after winter or cooling down from summer.

● Coldest place on Earth: Eastern Antarctic Plateau, Antarctica (as low as –94° C)
● Highest air temperature ever measured: 56.7° C at Death Valley, USA, 1913
● Twice a year, on the equinox, night and day are both 12 hours long the world over

Seasons

Weather System

■ Climate Crew

☀ An airborne factory where the weather is made
☀ Forms as winds swirl into regions of low air pressure
☀ Built from two weather fronts where warm and cold air meet

I'm the double-fronted phenomenon that makes Rain (and any other kind of weather, for that matter). I appear – out of thin air you might say – when air masses meet. I swirl into your hometown pulled along by an area of low Pressure, which sucks in air from all around. With me around, have no doubt, the weather is about to change.

You can see me coming! Look for a bank of cloud, thick at the base and fluffy up top. This is my warm front on its way, with a mass of warm air pushing up and over some colder air. The rising air will chill out and drop some light rain as it passes. After a brighter spell, my cold front shows up, with advancing cooler air pushing under the warm air mass. Prepare for a persistent downpour and – you never know – that rumbler Thunderstorm may put in an appearance.

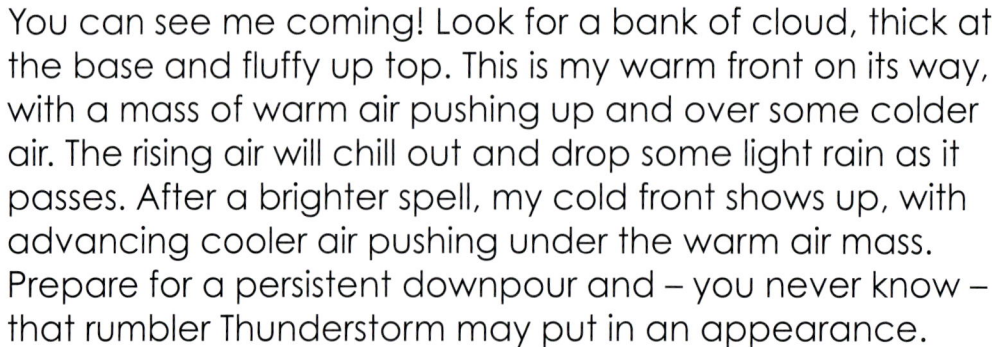

● In June 1995, 2.5 metres of rain fell in just 48 hours in Cherrapunji, India
● Warm fronts can reach speeds of around 45 kilometres per hour
● Cold fronts can reach speeds of around 65 kilometres per hour

Weather System

Climate

■ Climate Crew

✳ The long view of what is normal weather for a region
✳ Compares centuries of facts and figures to highlight extremes
✳ Generally, Earth is warmer the closer you get to the equator

We all know that weather has a habit of changing. Weather System rolls in day after day, bringing Wind, Rain, or shine. Through the year, Seasons like to change it up, too. Will winter be colder than summer? You betcha! Me? I'm all about the bigger picture on what the weather should be like in a place year after year after year.

You see, I'm a record of typical weather conditions, over a long period of time. I show that every region of Earth has a particular weather pattern and range of temperatures. The polar regions are cold, desert areas are dry . . . you get the picture? So when it gets hot and steamy in the Arctic or it snows in the Sahara, I'd say that's unusual – extreme, even – and I have to wonder if Climate Change has got something to do with it . . .

● In January 2018, 30 centimetres of snow fell in some parts of the Sahara desert
● In June 2021, the temperature of the Russian Arctic hit a record 38° Celsius
● The Amazon rainforest has had three droughts in the last 20 years

Climate

Climate Change

■ Climate Crew

✳ A shift in weather patterns made worse by humans
✳ Caused by gases that trap extra heat in the air
✳ A warmer planet will have more extreme weather

My pal Climate is right: I am the force behind extreme weather. No one invited me here, but you can't ignore me, so let me say a few words. I do what I do because you humans have added extra gases to the air – carbon dioxide from burning fossil fuels and methane from various industrial and agricultural processes.

Those gases take hold of heat, and Earth's atmosphere is warming up. The increase is small – about 1° Celsius in the last 250 years – but added up across the planet, it's a huge boost in extra energy. It's changing Climate and making extreme events like Flood and Drought happen. I'm a huge problem, but I can be fixed. You humans can start by using renewable energy that burns no fuels and planting vast forests to remove dangerous gases from the air.

● The amount of carbon dioxide in the air has gone up by half in 250 years
● Earth has become 1.1° Celsius warmer since 1880
● The world's temperature is rising faster now, at about 0.2° Celsius a decade

Climate Change

Climate Model

■ Climate Crew

✴ A climate-change prediction system powered by maths
✴ Uses data to show what weather happens where
✴ Vital in understanding when to expect extreme weather

I can see the future . . . sort of! I recreate Earth's atmosphere inside a computer and produce models to show how Climate Change might behave in years to come.

I divide up the atmosphere into many millions of spaces and give each one a set of numbers for things like air temperature, humidity and cloud cover. Next, I have some rules that control how each space is linked to its neighbours. If a space warms up, let's say, some of that heat is spread to the surrounding spaces just like in the real atmosphere. In this way, I can see how Drought and Heat Wave come and go across the globe. I can calculate a year's worth of Weather System's activity in a few hours, and figure out the weather for decades to come. Sorry to say, it looks extreme as far as I can see.

● Climate model supercomputers perform 14,000 trillion calculations a second
● Climate models divide the atmosphere into cells about 100 km square
● A climate model's computer program would fill 18,000 sheets of paper

Climate Model

Chapter 2
Windbags

Do you want to hear a story? It's about us, the Windbags. Mind you, you won't be able stop us once we get going. We just love to roar and whistle, howl and rustle. You hear that? We are air in motion blowing this way and that and all powered by our firm friend Pressure. On a bad day, we'll send in mighty Hurricane or Tornado, the biggest and meanest of our gang. Jet Stream is a fast friend, but stays above it all, never dropping in to say hello. But, sorry, we've been blustering along for ages now. What else can we tell you? Read on to find out!

Wind

Pressure

Jet Stream

Hurricane

Tornado

Wind

■ Windbags

☀ This flow of air is never seen but always noticed
☀ Created when air flows from high to low pressure
☀ Named after the compass direction of its origin

You've never seen me, but you all know it when I'm there, you feel me? Whoosh! From a gentle breeze to a full-blown gale, I'm a steady stream of air that has somewhere to be. Called into action by Pressure's changes, I flow from areas of high Pressure to those that are low. The bigger the difference in Pressure, the faster I move, as my air supply rushes in to make Pressure equal everywhere. I'm always named after where I've come from, not where I'm going – wherever that may be!

At my most extreme you'll find me in Hurricane and Tornado, and in colder zones I get a blast out of being a sting jet. This is a spike-shaped stream of high-speed air that leads to an extreme winter storm. If one's coming for you, be sure to stay out of harm's way.

● Anemometer: an instrument that measures the speed of the wind
● Winds swing to the right in the northern hemisphere and to the left in the south
● Roaring forties: fast-blowing westerly winds circling the globe near Antarctica

Wind

Pressure
■ Windbags

✳ This pushy type makes air move
✳ Works at the molecular level to create wind and weather
✳ A measure of the force of air in different parts of the sky

Gas molecules in air ping around in all directions and create a pushing force. I'm a way of measuring that. Packed tight, molecules push with more force (higher pressure). Spread out, they create an area of low pressure. Molecules move around to make pressure equal everywhere, which is why air always flows from high to low pressure, making Wind and Weather.

Pressure

● Measured in pascals (Pa) after Blaise Pascal, who discovered pressure (1650s)
● At Earth's surface, air pressure is about 100,000 pascals
● The lowest pressure ever recorded at Earth's surface: 87,000 pascals

Jet Stream

Windbags ■

- ✳ A never-ending river of air in the sky!
- ✳ High-altitude wind that circles the globe
- ✳ Creates strange weather out of season

Jet Stream

I'm a high-flyer. All weather is in the atmosphere's lower layer, made up of masses of air about 10 kilometres tall. I circle the globe by blasting along the boundaries between warm air masses and cold ones. I force Weather System to move with me, but Climate Change is pushing me into places I don't normally go, and whether I like it or not, I bring extreme weather.

- ● Jet streams are fastest in winter, reaching up to 443 kilometres per hour
- ● Polar jets bring cold weather in winter
- ● Tropical jets push warm weather up into cold places

Hurricane

■ Windbags

☀ A weather extremist that unleashes the biggest storms of all
☀ Windy and wet, it can create huge surges of ocean water
☀ Has a low-pressure centre – the eye of the storm

I'm a one-eyed storm monster that gets in such a rage and bluster you can easily spot me from space. I'm first seen in the hottest parts of the ocean, where warm air creates a zone of ultra-low Pressure. That creates a swirl of cloud banks that sets off across the sea, sucking up more heat and water vapour and growing ever larger.

When I hit land, I unleash a massive blast of Wind and Rain and can literally push the ocean up and over the shoreline. I take a rest while my empty central zone, the eye, passes overhead. Then it's straight back to buffeting and destruction. Hold on to your hats and everything else! Hurricane is my Atlantic name. In the Indian Ocean and South Pacific, I go by Tropical Cyclone, and in the North Pacific, you can call me Typhoon.

● A storm can be 9.5 kilometres tall and 650 kilometres wide
● Category 1 hurricane: winds above 120 kilometres per hour
● Category 5 hurricane: winds above 252 kilometres per hour

Hurricane

Tornado
■ Windbags

❋ A twisty air tube that brings the strongest winds on Earth
❋ This whirly funnel of dust links thunderclouds to the ground
❋ Often seen clustered in gangs called outbreaks

Sorry, I can't stop now, I'm all in a spin, but come along for the ride – if you dare! I'm the ultimate in extreme weather, a superfast wind system that's powerful enough to flip cars, rip off roofs and blow down city blocks, all in just a matter of minutes. Feeling dizzy yet?

You're most likely to see me in Tornado Alley, a strip of North America between the Rocky and Appalachian mountains, where conditions are just right for me. I form when a big Thunderstorm cloud drops down low enough to touch the ground. I make that connection as a swirling pipe of whirling wind that sucks air up into the monster storm above. You can't miss me, I stand out clearly in the sky as a dirty spout of dust. Keep an eye on me, my outbreak pals and I seem to be getting more extreme.

● The 2011 Super Outbreak in southeastern USA saw 322 tornadoes in three days
● Widest tornado: 4.2 kilometres wide (El Reno, Oklahoma, USA, 2013)
● A tornado out at sea is called a waterspout

Tornado

Chapter 3

Water Monsters

All life on Earth needs water, and we are here to deliver it. See those clouds? That's probably one of us on the way. How do you like your water? Wet Rain, fluffy snow, a short burst of Hail? The thing is, you can have too much of a good thing. Most of us are fine in small doses, but when we go extreme, we can cause real trouble. Worse still we might go missing, leaving nothing but dry and heat in our place. Climate Change says you'd better prepare for big changes coming your way, and coming soon.

Rain

Thunderstorm

Monsoon

Flood

Blizzard

Ice Storm

Hail

Rising
Sea Level

Flood
Defences

Rain

■ Water Monsters

- ☀ Liquid precipitation, aka drizzle, a shower or a downpour
- ☀ Carried by clouds that hover above land and sea
- ☀ Turns nasty when there is too much water to deliver

People often tut when they see me coming. They hide away, sheltering from my damp deluge. But I'm kinda essential for, you know, life on Earth. I return water to the land, to soak into the soil so that plants can sprout. I fill up watering holes for thirsty beasts to drink from.

It all starts when Sun warms up the oceans, making water vapour rise into the hot air. When the air cools, the vapour turns into cloudy clusters of liquid droplets. Eventually the droplets become so heavy that I appear, falling straight from the sky. The problem is, extra heat from Climate Change feeds me, creating wetter clouds, longer showers and sudden downpours that drench the land. If all my water doesn't fit down the drain, it just goes wherever it wants . . . my friend Flood will tell you more.

- ● World's wettest place: Mawsynram, India (average 1187 centimetres of annual rain)
- ● Most rain in one year: Cherrapunji, India, with 2647 centimetres of rain (1860)
- ● On 4 July 1956, a shower delivered 31 millimetres of rain a minute in Unionville, USA

Rain

Thunderstorm

■ Water Monsters

- ☀ A mega rainstorm that flashes and claps to get attention
- ☀ Builds the biggest clouds using steam and heat
- ☀ This natural danger is best respected

A grumbling rumbler, I appear with a crash and a flash. On hot, sweaty days, I put on a show of thunder and Lightning along with plenty of Rain and sometimes Hail. I'm quite the sight and sound! My flickering clouds loom higher than a mountain and have a menacing hammerhead look.

I grow large because warm winds whistle up through my middle, pulling in moist air that billows up as towering "thunderhead" clouds. The air swirling around my insides rubs against itself, creating an electric charge that makes sparks fly! Mighty Lightning strikes first, powerful enough to set trees on fire and to kill anyone in its way. Then comes my thunderous clap, rolling along later at the speed of sound. If you see and hear Lightning and thunder together, take shelter, for I'm right above you!

- There are 16 million thunderstorms across the globe each year
- Thunderheads can be 15 kilometres tall
- Seconds between lightning and thunder ÷ 3 = distance of storm in kilometres

Thunderstorm

Monsoon

■ Water Monsters

☀ A tropical weather system of two seasons – wet and dry
☀ Relied on by millions to water crops and fill rivers
☀ Biggest along the southern coast of Asia

I'm Wind and Weather System rolled into one, and I have a very important job. If I don't supply Rain at the right time of year, then Flood, Drought and even Wildfire take my place, making life very difficult for many millions of people. I hang out in the steamy, tropical parts of the world, where warm oceans meet the land.

I'm driven by differences in temperature on land and in the ocean. Each winter, the land is cold and Pressure is high, so Wind blows dry air out to sea. Come summer, it's all change! Sun warms the land up fast and Pressure drops. Soon wet Wind is blowing in from the ocean, bringing Rain – and lots of it. It fills the rivers and waters the fields. If Climate Change tinkers with my timings then who will water the crops at the right time each year?

● Monsoon systems: Indian, West African, Malaysian-Australian, North American
● Climate change is increasing rainfall during the Indian monsoon each year
● The North American monsoon occurs in NW Mexico, Arizona and New Mexico

Monsoon

Flood
■ Water Monsters

※ This deep destroyer shows up where it's not wanted
※ Causes untold wreckage wherever it goes
※ On the march along coasts and in big river valleys

When I rush in, I get the whole place soaking wet, gushing water into homes and drowning crops in their fields. Whether I creep up slowly or strike in a flash, I always leave a trail of destruction behind me. I'm no fun for anyone – a complete washout (geddit?)!

I'm what happens when too much water arrives in the same place at the same time. This is normally the fault of Rain falling in such extreme amounts that there is no time for it to drain away. Instead, water overflows and the streams and rivers spread out over low-lying land. I'm also seen when Hurricane arrives on land, along with a huge surge of seawater that splashes out along the coast. I'm really worried about Rising Sea Level. With that sort on the up, you'll be seeing a lot more of me!

● Bangladesh is the most flooded country in the world (up to 75 per cent some years)
● 60 centimetres of fast-moving water can sweep a car away
● In 2003, there was a flood in part of the Sahara desert

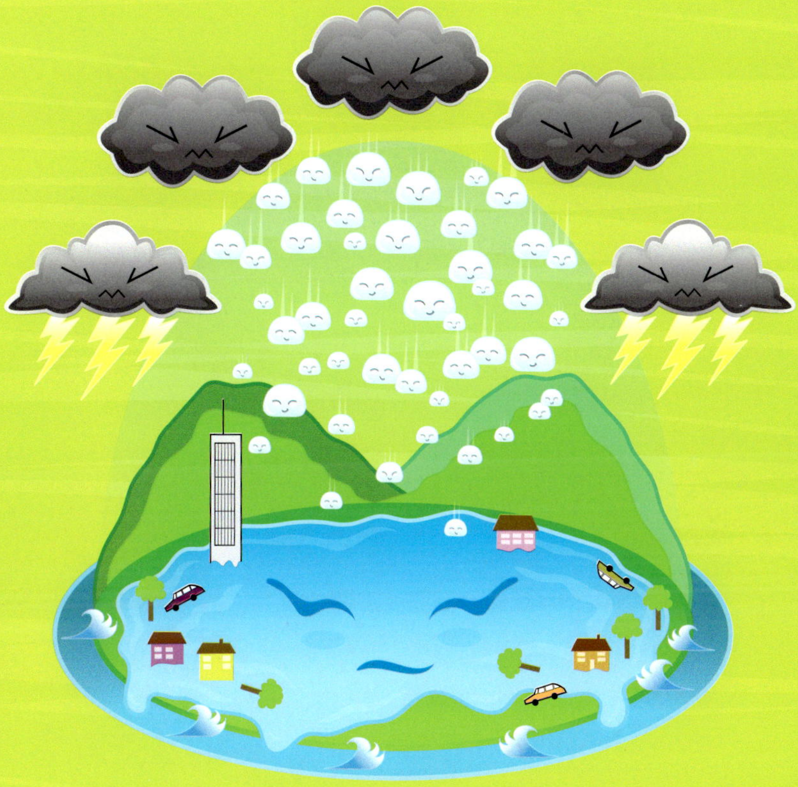

Flood

Blizzard

■ Water Monsters

✹ This swirling snow beast turns the whole world white
✹ A mix of cold wind and snow that builds deep drifts
✹ Can be a real hazard for humans

Part of me is supersoft snow but don't be fooled by the fluffy stuff. I'm really cold and make it hard for you to see. Working with Wind at its wintry worst, I turn gentle flurries of flakes into thick crystal swirls. Everything all around starts to look the same. Helped by Wind, I pile up snow into deep icy mounds but I'm a snow day no-no. Stow the sled, stay home, keep safe. Catch my drift?

Blizzard

● In 1972, a blizzard in Iran dumped 8 metres of snow in less than a week
● In 1993, the US "storm of the century" blizzard caused $5.5 billion of damage
● In 2021, a Texas snowstorm knocked out 69 per cent of the state's power supply

Ice Storm

Water Monsters ■

✳ This ice-cold attacker makes everything freeze
✳ Super-slippery type that makes paths and roads truly perilous
✳ A frosty response when very cold air sits beneath warm air

Ice Storm

Cold, quiet and often striking at night, I cover everything in shards of ice. I appear when dry air down low is below freezing, so the ground, trees and houses get very cold. Higher up, warmer, wet air drops liquid Rain. The raindrops freeze where they fall. Come dawn, eerie crystal coatings cover everything – even the roads. Best not to drive until Sun melts me away.

● An ice storm can make tree branches 30 times heavier
● In 2008, a state of emergency was declared in New England after an ice storm
● Ice storms coat roads in invisible – and very dangerous – "black" ice

Hail

■ Water Monsters

☀ This heavy type drops as ice from the sky
☀ Created by updrafts that blow raindrops to freezing heights
☀ Tours the world, even the warm parts

All hail me, as I send great balls of ice falling from on high! Bow down before me or, better still, get indoors, because this is going to hurt! You've met my cousins Rain and Ice Storm? Well, I am the mightiest of them all (I think so, anyway). My solid hailstones can be 15 centimetres wide (although they're normally about 5 millimetres). The largest ever recorded weighed 1 kilogram! No doubt I've made stones bigger than that, but they melt away so quickly, it's hard to know for sure.

My hailstones grow from specks of ice that are blown higher into colder air, adding layers of ice over and over. Eventually they become too big to stay aloft and down they go! I don't need cold conditions near the ground, so I am not uncommon in warm places, even deserts!

● The top speed of falling hail is 180 kilometres per hour
● Hailstones generally form above 6000 metres high in the atmosphere
● They can include grit and other debris sucked up by tornadoes

Hail

Rising Sea Level

Water Monsters

✳ A swelling of the seas caused by climate change
✳ Fed by hotter water and melting ice
✳ Even small changes will have huge effects in coastal zones

Thanks to Climate Change, the world is warming up and sea levels are rising. I may be a slow-moving complicated creature, but I'm a serious problem.

Sure, sea levels are always changing with the tides that roll in and out every day, but that's not me. No, I am the gradual rise of the sea as it moves higher up the land, little by little, year on year. This happens for two reasons. First, the ocean is getting warmer, and warmer water expands. Second, when ice on land melts, it adds new water to the seas. (Note: floating frozen seawater is melting too, but is not adding extra water.) I work slowly, but don't let that fool you. Flood Defences had better be ready. When Hurricane and extreme Wind coincide with my ever higher high tides, Flood is never far away.

● Half of all humans live within 100 kilometres of the ocean
● The ocean has risen by 20 centimetres since 1900
● If all of Antarctica melted, sea levels would rise by 58 metres

Rising Sea Level

Flood Defences

■ Water Monsters

✴ The first line of defence against rising seas
✴ Sometimes uses nature to absorb the shocks
✴ River barriers are employed to keep cities safe

Water, water, everywhere, but none shall get past us! We're here to counter Flood. You'll see us wrangling rivers inland and making a stand against the seas along the coast.

In an ideal world, nature will take the strain, giving floodwaters somewhere wild to go. Floodplains around rivers, for example, should allow excess water to soak away and bands of marshland and dunes along coastlines will help absorb ocean waves in a storm. But these strategies are not always possible because you humans like to build in these areas. So, we're here to engineer a response – tall sea walls and concrete dams that keep pushy water at bay. And for a city at the mouth of a river, a flood barrier with vast gates that click clunk into place will help block Hurricane's storm surge.

● Largest floodgate: Lake Borgne Surge Barrier, New Orleans, USA (1.6 km)
● One third of the Netherlands' Delta Works flood defence is below sea level
● Venice, Italy, is protected from flooding by 78 barriers that block high tides

Flood Defences

Chapter 4
Great Balls of Fire

We're too hot to handle and hard to fight against, but as the world warms up thanks to Climate Change, we're here to stay. Which do you prefer: a cold, wet weekend or a scorching, clear day? Think again! You may like it hot, but imagine it getting even hotter and staying like that day after day and night after night. That is what Heat Dome and Heat Wave have in store, coming soon every summer. Worse than that is Wildfire, which feeds off the scorched Earth destroying everything in its path. That's extreme, for sure. Things are hotting up!

Drought

Heat Wave

Heat Dome

Dust Storm

Lightning

Wildfire

Firefighting

Drought
■ Great Balls of Fire

✳ This dry type appears when it doesn't rain for weeks on end
✳ Destroys crops and habitats by starving them of moisture
✳ Creates long-term changes as entire regions begin to dry out

Rainfall is tricky stuff. Too much of it, and Flood starts gushing. Not enough of it, and in I creep, totally parched. I'm a lengthy period of time without a normal supply of water. I follow spells of clear sunny skies without Rain showing up. And I bring bad news. Soils dry out, plants wilt for lack of water and animals starve to death!

My problems run deep. When I invade a land, I make its soils thin and salty, bringing on Dust Storm. I make things so dry that there is no water to evaporate in the heat to make clouds that can drop water elsewhere. That means I spread even further. And if I happen too often, I can change whole habitats completely, with fewer plants growing back once Rain finally does show up. Forests become grasslands and grasslands change to deserts.

● The driest place on Earth is Antarctica. There's almost no liquid water, only ice!
● Not a single raindrop fell in Arica, Chile, between 1903 and 1918
● In Asia, a drought lasting from 1876 to 1879 led to 18 million deaths

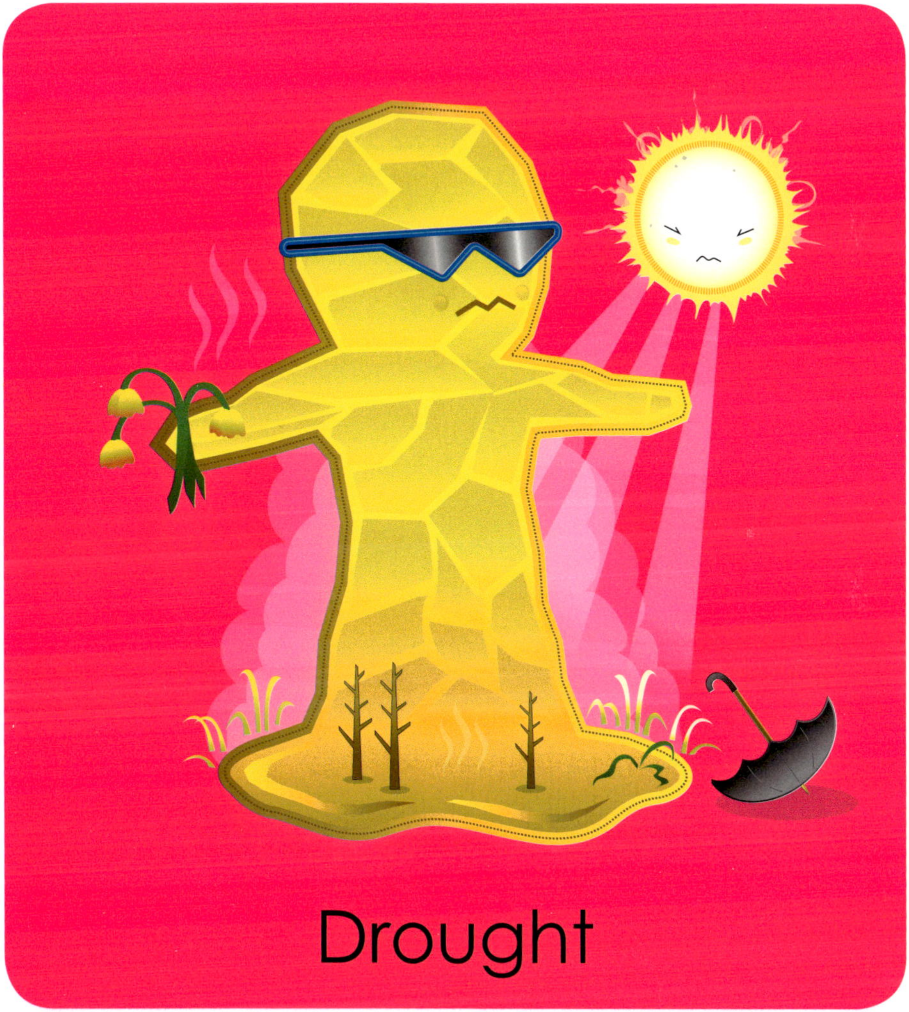

Drought

Heat Wave

■ Great Balls of Fire

❋ A time when days and nights are much hotter than usual
❋ This breath of hot, humid air makes life uncomfortable
❋ Extreme weather's biggest killer

It's getting hot out here, isn't it? I'm a stretch of time – just three days will do it – when it's hot, hot, hot day and night. Often my surge of heat comes flushed with an uncomfortably high humidity, where the warm air is also heavy with water vapour. I'm a real problem after dark, when the warmth stops people sleeping. Night after night, that makes me deadly.

Heat Wave

● Heat waves kill 5 million people each year
● Major US cities averaged two heat waves a year in the 1960s
● In the 2010s, major US cities averaged six heat waves a year

Heat Dome

Great Balls of Fire ■

* An atmospheric effect that traps hot air over land
* Extends heat waves and brings on drought
* Becoming bigger and meaner due to climate change

Heat Dome

Watch out, it's a trap! I'm a mass of high Pressure that keeps hot, scorching weather right where I want it. Down below, air cannot get out from under me, and fresh Wind is blocked from blowing in. I thrive on the big differences in temperature created by Climate Change. With me holding the hot air in one place, it means Heat Wave and Drought can do their worst.

● A heat dome can reach 6000 metres into the sky
● In 2021, a heat dome over North America created temperatures of 49° Celsius
● Under a heat dome, 50 per cent of crops can be damaged by sunburn

Dust Storm

■ Great Balls of Fire

☀ This grim type takes over when land dries out
☀ Fills with grit when stripping soils from farmland
☀ Signals that land is turning into desert

Even warm and dry places can be hit by heavy storms. But instead of Rain, I'll splatter and batter you with a dose of dust and specks of sand. I'm a common sight in deserts, where the soil is dead dry all the time. There, I have the job of shifting around the dunes from time to time. However, I also strike over farmland that has fallen into Drought's perilous grasp. The lack of rain has turned the soil to dust, and Wind whips it up and whisks it away. The fields are really blown away by me (geddit?)!

I'm especially fond of a Wind type called a gust front, where a downward stream blows along a wide area of flat land. You'll see what I mean, if we ever meet. The wind creates a thick wall of brown cloud. You can't miss it, it'll be a blast – for me, that is!

● A haboob is a wall of dust that is pushed along the ground by a downdraft
● Black Sunday, on 14 April 1935, was the largest dust storm in American history
● In 2021, a sandstorm took 13 days to blow across Mongolia, China and Korea

Dust Storm

Lightning
■ Great Balls of Fire

☀ Flashy fellow that electrifies the sky
☀ A powerful flow of nature's very own electricity
☀ A cause of wildfires, which are growing in frequency

Much hotter than Sun and bright enough to light up the night, I carry enough electricity to keep a light bulb burning for 18 months straight. I emerge after Thunderstorm's clouds have built up an electrical charge, and escape down to Earth as a gargantuan spark. My electrical flow heats the air into white-hot plasma and the air expands so fast that it breaks the sound barrier, creating a rumble of thunder across the sky.

Moving at 435,000 kilometres an hour, I'm the fastest thing in nature. Blink and you'll miss me. Be warned, though: you'll know about it if I hit you! Come summer, I like to work with my warm friend Drought to provide the spark for Wildfire. And due to Climate Change I'm getting more common in the Arctic. Feel the burn!

● Lightning strikes kill around 2000 people a year
● There are 3 million lightning flashes a day – that's 40 a second
● The Arctic had 7278 lightning strikes in 2021 (in 2014, there were less than 10)

Lightning

Wildfire

■ Great Balls of Fire

* A growing threat to wildlife and homes
* Driven by drought, wildfires can burn down forests in days
* This natural process is getting out of control

I'm gonna set the world on fire! Only joking! (Or am I?) Forests and grasslands catch fire from time to time. On the plus side, there are seeds that only sprout once they've been scorched and the ash from burned trees makes forest soils rich and fertile. But thanks to Climate Change, I'm becoming a dangerous extremist that can wipe out habitats and destroy towns.

I hang out with some real hotties. Drought makes a supply of dried wood and leaves – perfect fuel – then Lightning's spark sets it ablaze. Wind is my biggest fan, feeding the flames as I scorch vast areas at great speed. I'm burning hotter, faster and longer than is natural nowadays, and my smoke is often visible from space! Nothing much survives my touch and it takes years for the land to recover.

- A wildfire can burn at 800° Celsius
- Around 20 per cent of wildfires are started by lightning (people cause the rest)
- Black Dragon Fire (China/Russia, 1987) burned an area almost as big as Florida

Wildfire

Firefighting

✳ An attack on wildfire from air, land and sea
✳ Relies on a team of spotters to give an early warning
✳ Firefighters must clear one area of forest to save the rest

Watch out, there's Wildfire about. Summer is showtime and I have teams of forest wardens on the lookout for smoke signals. I use cameras, heat sensors and even satellites to watch for the next blaze. An early warning is essential. Wildfire can quickly grow out of control.

Fires in the wilderness are best fought from the air. Choppers and planes scoop up water from lakes and seas and dump it on Wildfire. Or they drop fire-clogging powders onto the flames. Even so, the fire can smoulder for some time and the slightest flicker can bring it back to life. So, I put boots on the ground and my brave firefighters cut firebreaks – wide gaps where all trees and plants have been removed. With nothing to burn, the fire stops there, and the forest (and towns beyond) are saved!

● Global SuperTanker: an aircraft that dumps 72,680 litres of water in 6 seconds
● The US Forest Service was set up in 1905 to help prevent wildfires
● In 2019, 7300 firefighters battled for six months against fires raging in Australia

Firefighting

Glossary

Air mass A vast packet of air of the same temperature and pressure that moves around the atmosphere as one unit.

Air pressure A measure of how hard air is pushing on anything it touches.

Black ice Clear ice covering a dark road. The see-through ice is impossible to detect but is very slippery.

Data A collection of measurements that can be used to describe what is happening.

Decade A period of ten years.

Deluge A sudden flow of water that covers the land.

Downpour Heavy rainfall.

Earth's axis The imaginary line around which planet Earth rotates every 24 hours.

Environmental To do with the natural environment.

Equinox A day when the length of the day is exactly equal to the length of the night. There are two equinoxes every year.

Fossil fuel A fuel is a substance that releases a lot of heat when it burns. Fossil fuels, such as coal and oil, are fuels made from the remains of ancient life forms.

Habitat The place where animals and plants live.

Molecular To do with molecules, the smallest parts of a chemical substance, such as water and the gases in air.

Plasma A superheated gas that is so hot that it glows and becomes electrified.

Strategy A complex plan that aims to achieve a big goal over a long period of time.

Tropical To do with the tropics, the warm part of the world close to the equator.

Water vapour The gas form of liquid water.

Watt A measure of power.

Weather front A place where warm and cold air meet, creating a change in the weather.

Wet season A part of the year in which there is a lot of rain.

Index

Main entry in **bold**